W9-DIR-642

THE
YALE SERIES OF YOUNGER POETS

HORIZONS

AMS PRESS
NEW YORK

Horizons

VIOLA C. WHITE

NEW HAVEN · YALE UNIVERSITY PRESS
LONDON · HUMPHREY MILFORD · OXFORD UNIVERSITY PRESS
MDCCCCXXI

Reprinted with permission of Yale University Press
From the edition of 1921, New Haven
First AMS EDITION published 1971
Manufactured in the United States of America

International Standard Book Number:
Complete Set: 0-404-53800-2
Volume 8: 0-404-53808-8

Library of Congress Card Catalog Book Number: 77-144715

AMS PRESS, INC.
NEW YORK, N.Y. 10003

ACKNOWLEDGMENTS.

GRATEFUL acknowledgment is made by the author to *The Atlantic Monthly*, *The Poetry Review*, "The Anthology of Magazine Verse for 1918" (William Stanley Braithwaite), *The Stratford Journal*, *The Survey*, and *The World Tomorrow* for permission to reprint in this volume certain poems which first appeared in their pages.

TO MY MOTHER

CONTENTS.

CLOUDS.

O CLOUDS that go to glory
In afternoon's clear blue,
From waterfronts of cities
I rise and follow you!
From springs that feed the forest,
From windy meadows' dew,
From pools of desert places
I rise and follow you!
From fallen rain, in fire
Caught up to heaven anew,
From living and from dying
I rise and follow you!

TO A SEA-GULL.

WINGED reconciler of the sea and sky,
Piloting winds that howl above the sun,
Riding the unenduring tides that run
To vex the sand with mutability,
Thou art the angel of ports never won
By proudest mariners that sail the sea,
Angel and sea-dog, winged with outland majesty!

O'er indigo depths where the palmtree crest
And tamarind from coral islands rise
Thou wert a spirit making Paradise
More beautiful for his divine unrest;
And where Icelandic kings with hoary eyes
And rudder colder than their ingot-chest
Steered poleward, thou wert there, a reveller and guest.

I watch thy domination of the air,
The level-winged and flashing silences
Through sunlit cloud and blue, ethereal ease;
And, having seen thee excellently dare
Lightning and hail, I wonder without cease
That ocean's dark necessity could bear
A freedom like to thine, valiant and poised and fair.

And now the sun is sinking down the deep
Thy wings are furled. Thy little fleet is spread
To rise and fall on long waves' crimson tread,
Outfloating Carthage. O'er earth's troubled sleep
Keep thou cold nightly vigil, and ahead
Of earth's incredible and awful sweep
Through unplumbed ether, ride upon the darkness steep.

WIND AND OCEAN.

Wind:

How long before daybreak, O watchful brother?

Ocean:

An hour or so. The sun shall rise
And my waves hail him even as when at first
The burning globe upon creation burst
They hailed him, with an ever-new surprise.

Wind:

I hold, with all-pervading sleep,
Earth's ward tonight.
The snake hides under a rock-heap,
The squirrel warms a hollow tree.
Panther and lynx hunt silently.
After a slow interval
Needles of the pine-wood fall
On rivers flowing out of sight.
How is it with thee?

Ocean:

Resigned in law, but not at rest.
Of the kingdom I possessed
Half rebels afar from me.
From my lair with graves I see
What has been moulding what shall be.
Over shelving coasts I tell
Creatures that change and do not hearken well
Of fate and of futurity,—
My memories their prophecy.

Volcanic cliffs rose in the north
At last night's sunset. I went forth.
Now the dark green waters swell
Over them, without a stir
White foam breaks and fades away
Amid the icebergs sluggishly.
There one stronghold have I bound
Against man, the voyager.

Wind:

The troubler and the mystery!
His bones I pasture through the wildernesses,
My dreadful sheep!

Ocean:

In the unfathomed depth of my recesses
His hostile ships a truce unwitting keep.
Strangest of animals! To gain the dowers
That in gods' hands beneficently burn
Of will and science, and their yielded powers
Against himself, a flaming curse, to turn!

Wind:

King of the void, heir of the dark, to inherit
From earth and sea
Compulsion that he names the Holy Spirit,
Like unto me!
(*A pause*)
How often, brother, we have held communion
In tolerant marshes, where rank, cluttered nests
Screamed round us, and in caverns myriad-eyed,
Encountering in tempest openly
And on the summit of emerging alps,
Before the race of man had come to birth!

Ocean:

Yea, and in tolerant marshes where rank nests
Scream round us, and in caverns myriad-eyed,
Encountering in tempest openly
And on the summit of emerging alps
We shall hold speech together when the name
And trace of man are vanished from the earth.

THE ASTRONOMER.

WATCHING suns and planets veer
Through the windless atmosphere
All night vigilant, alone,
He judged their going from a throne
Higher than kings of earth sit on,—
From the unbreathing midnight hour
Till the cold and raíny dawn
Struck the observatory tower
And pines began to bend and lower
On the mountain range below;
Herds dark-streakèd by the shower
Sought uplands green with melted snow;
The cataract in sheets of spray,
Sullen through the forest blown,
Through the forest drenched a way.
Then the stars of heaven were gone.
Fire-hearted steeds that run
With a heavenly delight
On the pampas of the night
Lawful and untameable,
All the stars from heaven were gone,
In his mind come down to dwell
From the pampas of the sky.
If they rise up clear and high,
If they set in blinding rain,
Of their ranging he can tell,
And they know their master nigh
When he strokes each plunging mane.
The celestial worlds inherit
The dark pasture of his spirit.

TO A FRIEND.

Night shall end my night,
Yet I trust
Thou art a thing too bright
To fall on dust.
The angel of the Lord
Shall lift thy sword,
Servant of the just!

Night shall end my night,
Yet I pray
Heaven spare thy light,
Lest lambs stray.
Thou remembering me,
Mine immortality
Lasteth all the day.

SUMMER THOUGHTS IN WINTER.

I GAIN the fireside from the whetted edge
Of January's moon, and icy ruts
That gleam the more to every whistling sledge;
And by the fireside, though wind yet cuts
Canyons without, my dreaming memory
Tells my numbed senses of green summer sedge,
While these, entranced, hear half believingly,
Even as if some hoar Neanderthal
Told cave-born children of the tropic mirth
His youth remembered, in the interval
Before the glaciers came down over earth.

Half dreaming I recall in mid-July
Motionless in a notch against the blue
A peak of dawn-red cloud, that, riding high,
When noon had stripped the spider webs of dew,
In shapes of white light manifold and deep
Had spread abroad and taken all the sky.
Crickets,—the voice of fields that talk in sleep,—
Were chirping, and the shadows of cloud sent
A changeful gloom across the fields. Afar
Out in the bay the sun that came and went
Flashed on one oar beyond the harbor-bar.

There was a highroad where through heaviest trees
The burning of the summer sun would dart
When they waved dusty leaves within the breeze.
Wheels passed; a laughing dog rode on a cart.
I struck out from the highroad, tangled soon
On paths that died in piney fastnesses,—
And there a bird sang all the afternoon.
Striving to reach the bird in hide-and-seek
I lost the bird, and in a hollow found
A pool, upon the brink a turtle sleek
That dived and blackly vanished without sound.

Can I believe that bees will yet grow bold
In the white buckwheat fields through August days?
That butterflies their yellow wings will hold
Rapt over sun-caked mud? That scrubby ways
Will turn for miles the air to ripening wine
Of berries, and the pods of milkweed fold,
As cast from heaven too soon, their armoured shine?
Alas, the time for summer dreams is past!
Alas for me that I must rise and go,
The world's death in my bones, against the blast,
Through the inertia of the fallen snow!

OCTOBER.

WITHIN the moving forest, where a shade
More brilliant than noon-light
Threw strangeness over friends, and fierce delight,
As through the lowering weather
They tramped together,
Upon the height
Of ledge on ledge up-piled, where bronze oaks cast
Their gusty moaning on the outland blast,
The winding-sheet of earth was being made;
And under the moist earth, made rich with meed
Of wind-swung falling nuts and leaves and casèd seed,
The dark mole burrowed and I found him not.
O'er multitudinous hills, with rapid tread
Muffled by heaped leaves dead,
I journeyed where
No mortal dwelling rose in cold gray air
Save an old smithy. One great wheel forgot
Leaned on the abandoned door. The windy hours
Led me by oozy flat and sudden gentian flowers,
Led me by hemlock path and by dim pools where rain
Fell in sparse circles all the long twilight.

In purple mountain-cleft a cider mill
Uprose. The last wood gods came trooping for their fill
With "Here's to you before the red sun drops"
Swilling the amber juice. From ram horns fell adown
The pale witch-hazel woven for a crown
With frost-cracked bittersweet on tossing locks.
Then they all turned and up the height did flee;
Stoning black butternuts from the grim gallows-tree,
Cramming their crops
With winter apples pecked by birds' departing flocks,
With tumult they were vanished in still rocks.
They left no trace. Only the lumbering bear
Left his track there,
He that was gone so deep
For hollow-caverned sleep.

Upon the farmland frosty morning broke.
    Blue forest smoke
Mile after mile was visible. The wains,
Loaded with hay, put wayfarers to pains
To give them all the road.
The fields with buckwheat stubble reddened wide,
The pumpkins stranded by a mellow tide
Lay amid sheaves of corn that, deeply bowing, owed
Some charmed obeisance not to be denied.
The air was blue, gray the horizon-range,
The sound of labor came distinct and strange,
And all the day I was unsatisfied,
Remembering vanished races.

Restless I wandered at the day's decline
By glassy river, and by vivid lake
Peopled alone by mounds the large ants make,
    Till at the last
Through silent streets bordered with elm I passed
That since the Revolution have not stirred
    Save at the flying bird,
Save at the fall of elm and maple leaves,
Like flickering memories. At the horizon-line
The sun through gathered cloud sent smouldering shine
Athwart the yellow, nest-revealing trees,
The grass yet green beneath, and glorious hill on hill.

    All through the night
I heard the floods and lightnings wreak their will
On earth. With an unbridled wind I sped
O'er half the world, and heard his awful pride
Broken in cemeteries, where he cried,
"I came not here to strive against the dead!"
    With rain I sank,
Blackening forest roots, down cold springs, dank
With drownèd leaves; down many a mountain-side
Widened in streams, tossing old tree trunks wide
Apart, and whirling them together, till
The streams plunged headlong in a river, fair

Advancing, flanked with palisades, to sea,
And prows of vessels pushed the massed leaves easily
Aside, while they steamed to the river mouth;
And on the banks, sudden from north, from south,
Fires leaped up as for a victory.

THE WITCH OF ALTHEMAIR.

When windless rain falls in the forest, making
        The green leaves move
Slightly, the drear lake's magic mirror breaking,
I stir and rise, remembering my love.
I see her grey eyes, threatening and fair,
I ride with her the stormy clouds above,
I sink in midnight flooding of her hair,—
        The witch of Althemair.

I know it is a dream; yet wildly hoping
        At some far sound,
I leave my poor hut, and on mountains groping
I seek her whom the age-long charm has bound
Within the hollow tree-trunk by her hair
About the tree-trunk wound and interwound,
Her dark hair where the rains are falling there,—
        The witch of Althemair.

I keep on earth my travail for a token
        When the rains fall,
That with an ecstasy no time has broken
I rode the height of heaven at her call.
While mountaineers draw round their pine-knots' flare
I seek the stormy forest and the pall
Of night by night that darkens with her hair,—
        The witch of Althemair.

PERNEB.

[*Perneb's tomb has been set up in the New York Metropolitan Art Museum.*]

PERNEB built himself a tomb.
Round the wall go slaves a-row,
Slaves with sidelong red feet slow,
Staring frontward with their eyes,
Bringing Perneb through the gloom
Of his solemn, spicy room
Thousand loaves and joints of meat,
Thousand live gazelles or so,
Thousand trays of figs and wheat.
Following them in a line
Slaves bear out of dim recesses
Perneb's change of thousand dresses.
Perneb has no dearth of wine.
Through the high and breathless air
Red and yellow jars shine bare,
The blue lotus flowers twine
Accurately, in design.
At the centre, large and wise,
Painted Perneb doth arise,
Reviewing his processional,
Counting cattle on the wall
Opposite, each flank appraising.
Perneb with a swelling chest,
Perneb with a chastened waist,
A gold collar interlaced
With the scarab, and a wig,
Holds a folded linen cloth,—
Sole concession to mutations,—
To flap wingèd insects off.
Sons and wives and poor relations
Kneel before him, under size.

Unless all that's left us lies,
Perneb was a chamberlain
Administering for a king

Who appreciated him.
He arrayed his Memphian king;
He inspected cattle, too,—
Had a priest's job on the side,
When he wore the leopard skin.
Shudderingly thought has tried
To contemplate that land's descent
Down the abyss, when Perneb went.

Where's the eye that made the slaves
Cower in arrested waves?
Where's the hand that flapped at flies,
And kept relations under size?
Where's the will that laid on stone
Shape for twice two thousand years
By commandment of its own,
That so and not otherwise
The decorous chambers glow
For no reason man can know
Save that Perneb willed it so?
Sands of dusty years have strown
Abu Roash and the south,
Sakkara and Dahsur's drouth.
Twice two thousand years are blown
Harmlessly as yesterday
O'er the walls of Perneb's sway.

In the chamber toward the west
Lies a skull like any skull
Neutral, indisputable,—
Perneb's,—so it may be guessed.
Desert thieves dispersed the rest
From the dwelling clear and fit.
Time's a tactless thing at best.
Perneb got the worst of it.

DANDELION.

DOWN the road I spied the weed,
And the head was gone to seed.
I ran to blow it into air.
Suddenly from out the heart
Sighed a ghost, complaining there:—

"I am bound in a world that is old and round
    And cannot die,
Though it wave perpetually,—
Hoary-headed world and round
That debars me from the sky.
In a solid ball imbound
    Captive evermore I cry."

Then I pulled the stem and blew.
Out upon the wind he flew.

FULL MOON ON THE ACROPOLIS.

HERE is the immortality of night.
Time, tranced to marble quietude, forgets
Futurity. The wind has dropped stone-cold
To sleep on level vineyard, Attic plain
And gulfs smooth and moon-cloven. Flocks and herds
Move fitfully along the darkling slopes.
A soldier's ballad, sudden, rough and free,
The crowing of a single cock, beguiled
With infinite effulgence of false dawn,
Ephemerally have surprised the night
Like shooting stars that fade upon its heart.
Borne to reality of solemn arch
And radiant architrave and pillars reared,
Blinding with old day, from the earth to heaven,
Have I outwatched the track of hollow ship
And track of chariot, where sea and plain
Stretch naked to the consummated moon.
The lights of Athens, proud and myriad,
That seem as just about to move along
Processionally, and that yet remain,
Are tongues of fire round the city's sleep
Syllabled by the dead that speak in light
Instantly clear.

For yet a little while,
Evading despot reason's sentïence
Called time and space, I have come back again.
Seaweed apparent in the early gulf,
Mysterious with distance, comes my hope,
My grave-deep fantasy. Miraculous,
Arcana-archèd city, nevermore
Of Theseus nor of Hadrian, and thou
Acropolis appointed desolate
As God Himself o'er the loquacious earth,
Where is the dawn of old? For I recall
It raced in gold upon a racing sea,
In burning gold upon the wine-red sea,
An ardent charioteer, from unshored deeps

To Phaleron's blue coast, and far within
The haunt of wind-vexed reeds. Day broke so clear
On the religious town that the frail mists
Shone rose-red, beyond light; immaculate
And Cytherean, from her airy ocean,
The Parthenon emerged from rose-red mists.
I stood where yet the Propylaean gate
Was not swung open to receive a throng
Brave in the sunlight. Priest and lutanist,
Elder and warrior, those bearing trays
One after one; advancing in a file
Those bearing water vessels; cavalry
Wind-footed and compelling as the wind,
And arrow-thoughted youth, for government
Trained in assembly neath judicial stars,
Awaited. Maidens, moulded for the clasp
Of starry gods that set memorial
Of beauty constellated in the sky,
Were leading deep-browed heifers with the tread
Of sandal-fastening Niké. Yet amid
The holiday, premonitory fear
Was on me, for I felt my forehead cold
With Proserpine's unearthly asphodel,
Blasted by too much moonlight. I remained
Half dreaming. As one bodes from swallow flight
The fall of empire I blamed the gift
Of votive offering forgotten for
This swift eclipse of day, and homeward turned
To lift from scented wood the honey-bread,
The Cretan wine, the kneaded cake, prepared
Of blossoms from whose pollen bees fed not,
So early were they plucked. Even as I turned
One warned to hasten, and I mocked at him,
"The citadel will be as Ilion
Doubtless, when I return,"—whereat a shout
From myriad throats like a young eagle rose
Aloft the height, to swayless forests of
Vast-shapen gods in august conference.
Borne on the wings of that victorious shout

I passed along the highway where urned death
Upraises shapes of bright life's commonplace*
To lands where death was prototype of life,
Where generations kept with scourge and sword
Memorial of the god that harrowed hell
For healing of the nations that yet groan.

It is unfitting that a mortal thought
Should outlive deity. I would my thought,
Hid in deep-rivered hills, had shared the life
Of mines as yet unquarried to the sun.
Pale centuries are dead. I have returned,
Haloed and blinded with the selfsame dream,
Past all that mortal men have reared in prayer,—
(Gigantic guesses through the wilderness),—
Argos-eyed hope, superincumbent fear
Devoted as its prey, to Attica
Possessing in the hollow of her hills
A brilliant slumber, rapt ineffably.
Around it pepper-trees like fountains wake
Selene's silver silent light to sound.
Hymettos hath forgot his heavy bees,
Pentelic slopes are stretched like perfect limbs
Of some forwandered giant night o'ertook,
And fane-crowned Lykabette, arising, strikes
His mitred head amid the glancing stars.
Orestes, Christ and Mahomet passed here.
A little stone remains; the ether shines
As when a thunderbolt, departing, leaves
Memorial night, with all its silences.
Olives coeval with philosophy,
My thought turns marble-cold! I question not,
Nor ponder overmuch how these gray leaves
Have waved the sage asleep. Long grass that runs
Oblivious of wrong o'er living word
And lost word, wrought alike by dead men's hands,
I question not nor supplicate again!
Acropolis that change has left divine

*Dipylon.

And inarticulate as will of gods
Half-shaped from hollow cliff or haunted run
Or water, I nor question overmuch
Nor supplicate, for all my thought is turned,
Through vigil and the moon's plenipotence,
More multiform than marble, and more cold.

THE PREHISTORIC LAKE.

When the hamlet and the dogs are sleeping
The green caverns of the mountain quake;
Rows of old men come at midnight, weeping,
Weeping for the legendary lake.
To and fro they interlace the moonlight,
To and fro with stately rhythm glide,
All together to a mournful measure
Piling old runes in a massy treasure
Round the oak roots of the mountain-side.
Then before the morning's eyes
View that trancèd sacrifice
They have vanished to the caverns where the water courses rise.

Swift the chattering and bright
Little hamlet shakes the night
From its heels when larks awake,—
Not a peasant in it caring
As he whistles on his faring
If, beyond a granddam's knowing,
Where sunburnt feet and scythes are going
The transparent waves were flowing
Of a legendary lake;
If leaning palaces and trees
With grey moss clinging at their knees
Gazed in those blue deeps, forsooth,
At dawn, remembering their youth,
Or kings in robes like chrysolite
Shining through the summer night
Their blameless covenant did write.
Jacques, a-bowing neath his rake
That combs the brown leaf from the grass
Beside the road folk take from mass
Shakes his scraggling beard in ruth
At the legendary lake,
And the Evil One's deceiving
For a pomp that never was.
Is it matter for believing
That, where the Father's dwelling be

And every night the Father pours his tea
Shining monsters, fixed of eye,
Swam passing one another by?
And the iridescent glass
Boys dug rumbling out of the ground,—
Bowls and baubles to a rumbling sound,—
Were the Evil One's deceiving
For a pomp that never was.
Not a coney skin he'd stake,
Not a yellow straw, in truth,
On the ruined forest hoary
Or the cross-unhallowed glory
Of the legendary lake.

PAST AND FUTURE.

Future speaks:

Seldom I honor the dark wife
Appointed me for bale or bliss.
No bounds are set upon our strife;
The present is our fleeting kiss.

Her passionate will has made me halt.
Her triumph is my lost desire.
On stairs of marble and basalt
She holds me down a burning fire.

We two shall walk the earth at noon
And when the sun is lying dead.
Our way beneath the sun and moon
Inevitably lies ahead.

Our way with outcast gods is seen,
August, but by calamity.
Her head is bowed for what has been,
And mine for what will never be.

IMPRESSIONS OF HAWAIIAN MUSIC.

I. The Rising Moon.

A Malayan runs his canoe over the lagoon,
Over unfathomed waters black and calm,
Kept by the alligator and the loon.
He slides ashore, and climbing arm over arm,
Goes climbing to the top of the highest palm,
For the topmost leaf to work his enemy harm,
Gathered at midnight, brewed in the witch doctor's charm.
What is it there,
The yellow glare
Swinging out of the sultry air?
Is it the lynx that hunts by night,
His fixed eye watching there so bright
For the brown body descending soon?
The feathery top of the tallest palm
Sways in alarm,
Violently the palm top sways to the rising moon.

II. The Curse.

At dawn when dew shook heavily
And islands laughed within the sea,
My neighbor claimed my banyan tree.
Through sun and shade till spacious noon
I cursed him softly to a tune
Of wild, compelling melody:
I watched through the still afternoon
My neighbor's tongue becoming thick,
My neighbor growing very sick,
And dying most unquietly;
Then, when the sun sank in the bay
Upon the bright and cloudless day,
Myself, my wife, my children three
Had salad from the banyan tree.

III. After Rain.

The light is set on the hill,
The stream runs fierce and free.
I am cold with the tears of forests chill
As I come to thee.

The light is lost in the night,
The stream is lost in the sea.
Through forests weeping in bright moonlight
I come to thee.

THE CHILDREN AND THE INLET.

We must be starting to explore.
Our boat will leave the lake, and quite
Vanish out of people's sight.
The border willows twist and curve
Around one half of the lake shore,
Making no deeper bend nor swerve
Where the stream comes rushing in
From the dark and watchful wood
Than in many a shallow more.
Unless you knew you never could
Find the place. Here we begin,
Pushing the willow boughs aside
That hide the mouth, now we have pried
Oars out for paddles, for the space
Narrows. We grind our teeth and brace
Our feet and paddle hard and quick,
Blaming each other when we stick,
Inch after inch upstream. A tree
Stands in the water. With a clank
Our boat chain lassoes it, lest we
Go slipping backward in the chase.
Inch after inch we push along
The current, obstinate and strong,
Splashing and shoving manfully.
Look how it winds and winds about!
But we have come to track it out.
The asters crowd down to the bank
And monkey-face looks in to see.
The woods close round us large and black.
It is about time we went back.
Now let her go,—and all we do
Is take life easy, sit and steer
While grandly we go sliding through
The landscape back and backward,—when
We shoot out in the lake again!
We did not know it was so near.
We come out blinking into it,
And there the fishermen still sit

Just as we left them, in the sun,
And the golden ripples run
On the lake floor fast and clear.
Things do not seem so different
From what they did before we went.

AT THE SCHEIDEGG.

Come up, come up, come high enough and free
To match your strong heart with the eagle's wing,
And come a-chasing after spring,
White and green, a lovely thing.
Or did you think that spring was fled
Like a dryad in a tree
In July's maturity?
Or did you think that spring lay dead
To the locusts' litany?
O, follow where the spirit led,
When a silver-dripping morn,
Sudden witch, around you spread
The lake-leaning alders red,
When on your devoted head,
Dreaming of outriding ships
From the sea's apocalypse,
The last wind of winter sent
Star-dust snow, and wonderment.

Come up, for airs are breathing glad and fine,
The rocks climb sunward all in burning gold!
Come up! Upon the edge of the snow-line
That marks the pale lands' uttermost decline
And green's contested splendor of ascent
A bird goes dropping as he flies divine
Reveillé bold,
Evanishing aloud
In an inspired cloud;
And very far below the valleys keep
The sultry calm of their midsummer sleep,
And far above the blue-caved glaciers go.

Here bloom the flowers of a haunting bride,
The buds half-seen before the rainbow died
That scattered here her skiey laughters low.
Where the streaked snow drips earthward in pure light
Are wide-eyed crocus, lavender and white,—
The excellent awakening of snow,—

And violets pulled from the Alpine glow,
And furred hepatica, whose color vies
With the cupped glory of the hyaline
When, kneeling at sunrise,
An angel lifts within his hands its shine
Against the slanting sun, a tremulous grail and sign
Here mystical and still
Across the resurrected summit chill
Is borne the cry unutterably hurled
From walled ice-caverns of another world,
The secret three times purified in dew,
The ranging presence, virginal and new,
Of glory uncreated. Even as Truth
Arises out of windy Memory,
Spring and first youth
Come over the abyss triumphally.

SNOWSTORM.

THERE lives above in a lonely place
A maiden, free as the winds are free.
Snow-white are her arms, snow-white her face,
She tosses her white thoughts carelessly;—
Falling showers of snow,
Purely and perfectly free,
Lightly and airily blowing
For mortals to see,
She tosses her perfect thoughts
Carelessly, carelessly.

JUNGFRAU.

JUNGFRAU is a resting cloud,
Or a Lorelei of snow.
Over her the moon has bowed
With a lake-like murmur low.
Troops of the night hours wing
O'er the maiden and the fay,
Rapt and spiritual thing!
All the night her summit white
Glimmers in an endless day.
Round her dazzling winds cry loud,
And she is more glad than they.

DUTCH SLUMBER SONG.

THE little fields are very green,
And kine the little fields do keep.
Through many channels laid between
Waters creep.

A stork goes stepping unto nest,
Goes stepping solemn like a king;
And red the west, and in the west
White gulls wing.

Boats are floating all the night
Down the level waters black,
Boats that left by candle-light
Have all come back.

They have cut the hay and bound it.
Poled along, the barge lags by.
Lazy duckweed winds around it
Lingeringly.

Fishers squatting in a row
Now have told their latest tale,
Now the flapping mills swing slow,
And words fail.

Goodnight, little fields so green,
Kine that little fields do keep,
Little country, brave and clean,
Half asleep.

FAIRY MESSAGE.

You still might harken on the hills
To roundelay
Of elf song gay
And figures flying on the wind when moonlight nights are clear,
Heighho for fairy laughter, if you had ears to hear!

And in the dewdrop you might trace
Our rainbow wings,
And chance on rings
For woodland dance, moss-couched, and each alight with fire-
flies three,
Heighho for fairy laughter, if you had eyes to see!

Then weep no more in mournful melody
A vanished race
Whose dwelling place
Shines at your feet, and evermore remains a happy land,
Heighho for fairy laughter, if you could understand!

SUNDAY MORNING.

THROUGH deep heaven's intense blue,
Over grain fields bowed with dew
The bell in the white church-tower tolls
Summons to accustomed souls.
Folk go by in twos and threes
Under the full-leafèd trees
Of the central village street,
In their best, stiff and complete,
With hushed stir. Their words are slow.

They are past. Now swiftly grow,
Moss in hollow pear-tree croft,
Cricket song in hid hayloft!
An old spider floats out free,
Borne along invisibly.
In and out the hollyhocks
Bees go moving the tall stalks.
Pollen-dusted out they creep
With hum that lulls silence asleep.
The old-fashioned garden glows
As though jewels of the mine,
Sighing souls out for repose
Of waving air and garden-close,
Hither came all hot to shine.
Poppies purple, white and red,
Swift and fragile flame have spread.
Zinnia and marigold
Spring's blithe hardihood unfold.
Here are the blue sailors, and
Indigo of Samarcand,
Coreopsis' fiery stars
Made to flash on scimitars,
Gold laburnum, brilliant phlox
Some pied elfin shepherd leads
Teasingly through haunts of weeds;
Portulaca's sun-cupped wine
Like the draught of youth divine;
Columbine, lorn for bare rocks

And solitary water-spring;
Four-o'clock, unwakening;
Basil of old tragic story,
Mignonette, and morning-glory
Thin-misted with the breath of dawn.
A yellow rambler-rose swings on
The gnarled trunk of an agèd pine,
High and higher up to twine,
Till on branches buds are seen
Laughing with the evergreen
Like a mystic's glad and free
Dream of immortality.

Past the garden is a shed.
All around it junk is spread,—
Tools that ought to spade or hew
Or cut, yet never did, nor do,—
Things hacked out ere rise of sun
And mercifully left half done.
Rank and lush the weeds abound
Over the outlawèd ground.
Ragweed, pigweed, burdock show
Higher than a man can grow.
The few vagrant garden seeds
That spring up are choked by weeds.
The wild grape and the red lily,
Watchers on abandoned farms,
Sleep here in each other's arms.
Jewel-weed shakes gleaming, chilly
Dewdrops to the wind. Bee-balms,
Thistle and day primrose thrive
Over a forgotten scythe.

Ho! I thought that all the people
Were in church beneath the steeple.
There's another loiterer.
An old man sits at his door
Bowed and motionless and hoar.
Full of years he seems to be

As I am of heresy.
Year by year he strove with stones,
Weather, weeds, and insect-blight,
Rising up by candle-light,
Swinging scythe at sultry noon,
Sometimes under the cold moon.
Now he feels it in his bones.
Mild blue eyes he has, and vast
Beard. The village life goes past
Where he sits before his door
Bowed and motionless and hoar.
I know not what things he sees
Over the unmoving trees.

IN THE COW PASTURE.

THE mortal hurry drops from me.
I am a brown beast, kind and slow.
Along uneven paths I go
And nip a young thorn-apple tree.
I do not care to move at all
When sudden thunder-showers fall,
Pasturing ruminatively.

THREE HOURS AT OWEGO.

THE planks upon the bridge are old,
And clatter when a team goes by.
Between them here and there a bold
New plank rears up and takes the eye.
Midway a pedagogic man,
Leaning over, stoops to scan
Streaming water weeds that spread
Green in Susquehanna's bed.

Passing by I come to town,
Where in the mid-morning hush
Houses steadily look down
On dewy lawns and dim smoke-bush.
Here storekeepers say you nay
In a suave and stately way.
Here notes sweet and wavering
Fall from some child's practising.

Could I but linger year by year,—
And even now the train is due,—
I would build a castle drear,
I would build a homestead too,
And the masking ivy leaves
Should cover battlements and eaves
Till none but nesting birds might see
Their dissimilarity.

SEPTEMBER WALK.

A LEVEL stretch lies on ahead.
Shivering we quit the forest shade
Where puddles stay undried and brown mushrooms are made,
For bushes flowering in hot sun
And the bees working over them.
Goldenrod with sweet-fern grows
Upon the right; the oat fields spread,
And buckwheat. A few apple trees
Stand in grain up to their knees,
Dropping round them gnarly fruits.
Beyond the fields a river flows
Calm amid the mountains' pride.
I might be looking on the right,
But on the left a dirt bank goes
Straight up to blue sky, and I see
Water dripping from the roots
Of shrubs atop it,—such a sight
As if the ground cracked suddenly
By commandment of a jinn
And I saw what the woodchuck sees,
Without the toil of digging in.

THE SAGE'S BOAT.

I TAKE my boat out in the cloudy morning to ponder on truth.
Over the lake stirred by faintest undulations
I row silently
Among stumps topped with coarse grass
And logs lengthwise in the water
Rotting, covered with moss.
I pass over red and yellow reflections
Of trees, red and yellow, that come down to the lake edge.
Willows and cattail rushes
Stand out in the water to meet my boat.
I float shoreward over lily pads.
The cattail rushes close about the boat,
Waving over my head.
A wind stirs their tops,
Leaving the willow leaves motionless.
I see the cattails reflected, clear and mysterious, in the water,
And the image of the white sun of heaven.
I ponder on truth ultimate and imageless,
But I cannot grasp it.
I think in the images about me,—
The cattails reflected in the water
And the image of the white sun of heaven.

PRISONERS.

We rise not up to wonder of wingèd mirth,
We bow not down to the ground's abysmal prayer,
O birds like resurrection over the air,
O meek and lowly dead, possessing the earth!

NOCTURNE.

We have given our hearts to the Beast, for the Beast to share,
The stealthy-footed patrol of the city street.
Custom his name, and tame all his ways and sweet,
Though blood yet drips on the chartered pavement fair.
Not as the conquered, flinging to ancient air
Hearts more free than their fiery winding-sheet,
We have given our hearts to the Beast, for the Beast to share,
The stealthy-footed patrol of the city street.
Long his hunger as an avenging prayer,
While we, crying out where the midnights meet,
Mark the pacing of those majestic feet
With the recurrence of never-evaded care.
We have given our hearts to the Beast, for the Beast to share.

THE SEARCH FOR THE WILL.

A LADY exquisite and old
Lies beneath the shadowy gold
Canopy, about her head
The cold patience of the dead;
And the lady's maid beside
Watches, breathless and wide-eyed
At each far-off murmuring,
Like some hunted forest thing
Without a friend or a pretence,
Whose dumbness is its one defence.
The physician now has gone
And the rector soft withdrawn,
Nothing left to say or do.
What are these come stealing through
The trancèd house, from room to room
Peering, troubling the rich gloom,
Till by different doors they reach
The silent chamber, without speech
Confronting one another, eyes
Averted, with a pale surprise?
Sudden explanations break
From all. With dignity all make
It evident they could not rest
When their relative's request
Had called them hither,—they had come.
The lady's maid sits frozen dumb.
Each one, shrugging doubtfully,
Starts upon a specialty,
With incredulous, veiled looks.
One proceeds to search the books,
Turning leaves and scattering
White light through the chamber dim.
One bends with assurèd air
Above the old and carven chair
Of the watcher by the bed,
Whispering. She shakes her head.
One, aghast and tremulous,
Vexed with himself he should be thus

When the rest have equal claim
To a supernatural blame,
Holds his wife's effects, while she
Flings the jewels restlessly
From their dark Etruscan case,
Strews the gowns of dewy lace
And sunset cloud about the floor,
Fumbles for a secret door
Behind the portrait frame, that, stirred,
Groans almost a spoken word.
And the lady keeps her state,
High, and yet inviolate,
Like a halo round her head
The cold patience of the dead.

THE LAKE ON MY LANDS.

MASTER of rolling plains, to sow and reap,
Master of timbered mountains, that rise up
One after other till they only cease
At the command of time and space, to which,
Master of many lands, I bow as they,
I have no lordship of my mountain lake.
It is not even measurable to me.
Asking upon the brink, "O, what am I?"
I lean above the surface. The clear lake
Gives, with the calm directness of a child,
My image, in abundant green of trees
And quiet blue commingled, and the flash
Of wingèd dragon fly. All these it holds
Upon the surface, and the depths move not,
Remote and imageless and ocean-deep.
Should the lake ask of me, "O, what am I?"
I could not answer; for I hollowed not
The cleft that goes down far as the mountain towers,
In which the stainless water lies asleep.
What titan agony or young despair
Of earthquake shock, or what descending glacier
Passed, with enduring imprint, I know not;
Nor how long since, what far and savage night
When herded wolves froze under a bright moon,
The water, pouring in, possessed its home.
The lake was never thought nor formed by me.
It lies, the confidant of heaven's delight.
Swallow and wind upon the surface pass,
And water beetles take their crooked way,
And lilies slow and radiant unfold.
To each what each desires, but to me
Wondering about the depth, it gives no sign.
I might sink in it, yet I could not plumb
The waters. Below accident they wait
Certain and imageless and infinite.
I thought the sun would send a final path
Of light into my lake. The sun looked down,
And looked upon the lake most gloriously,

But, blind in his essential burning, gazed
But little distance in. The depths remain
Secret and imageless and infinite.
And in the lake the moon from a steep throne
Viewed her own solitude with awe, and passed
Upon her wingèd throne. The depths remain
Patient and imageless and infinite.

LIBERATED.

"Why dost thou watch the lotus-bloom all day,
Thou who hast come so short a road, yet weary?
Why, when the hills with whirling snows are dreary,
Dost thou go leaping like a stag at play?"

"Sources of streams rolled underground, mysterious
As mighty-armed and waning kingdoms' care,
Sources of braggart dynasties, imperious
Over the jackal and the empty air,

"Long have I traced. I soared above and under
The wheel of things that breaks whatever is,
Ahasuerus-like; and wilt thou wonder
I love the lotus more than maiden's kiss?

"I that have watched Mnemosyne a-sleeping
And angel Lucifer hurled down the height,
Where is the wonder that I go a-leaping
With lonely stags, against the winter light?"

CHILD OF ADAM.

I WAS the rock
Warm or cold as sun came or went,
I was the oak
And boughs grew out of me,
I was the lake, reflecting early light,
Ages ago. The event came between,—
Dark, estranging, mighty, ineffable,—
Between me and my brothers so innocent and sure.
No sign of it dwells in the caverns of ocean,
No mark of it on hills unscalably divine.
What was it that could isolate a race,
That, all the source grown mythic, yet can drive
Me through rejoicing May, a bowed and contrite man?

FAILURES.

THEIR rightful fate has turned them down.
They will not have a substitute,—
From driving wagons through the town
Descend to grind horse-radish root.
If they wear not the coronal
They'll starve before they strive at all.
The old professional allure,
Decreasing friends, makes want secure,
Until with pride of specialty
They have attained to misery.

And some, like rock beneath the sun
Or weeds or earth or heavy rain,
Are elementally begun,
But never ended or made plain;
Forever promising a spring
They hint of resurrectioning.
They have no thought of time, like trees.
Not so far different from these
The interrupted seers, bowed
And sullen, from lightning of a cloud.

The ardent spirits in the throng
Of care-worn toilers, with a mind
To roar while tracking down the wrong
That is let slip by sleeker kind;
The folk whose phantasies give birth
To wrong that never was on earth,
Alike apportioning their blame
Prophetically fare the same.
As swift as in Jerusalem
Their days of leanness follow them.

Herein are the conservative
Old votaries of seven sins;
Herein the lotterists who give
Their venture to the man that wins;
And they whose lives are different

For the constraining past event
That set the boundary for aye.
The born spectators of the play
Through half-closed eyes' insouciance
Herein observe the puppet-dance.

It is a disenchanting wine
That these will drink unto the end,
Who have nor human nor divine
Approval where the hills descend.
I know not of what Circe's cup
The children of good fortune sup,
What incantations therein flow
That all alike those children grow.
I pray God keep me from success,—
My only answered prayer, I guess.

THE GUARDIANS.

When step by step fate beats me farther back
Until I stand upon the ultimate,
It is not will nor instrument I lack
To put myself beyond the spoils of fate;
Nor duty to a Maker that made ill,
Nor judgment from the lips of living men,
Nor end of what I only might fulfil,
Nor pain of endless doom arrests me then.
I hold my sword because, the chasm past,
I fear the encounter with those mighty dead
That made each bloody slope unto the last
A pasture-land where climbing flocks are fed.
I fear lest they come, vast and justified,
With mute, appraising eyes,— and turn aside.

THE FIRST POPPY.

O SHAKEN scarlet, vauntingly alone
Under the sun,
One love there is like thee, and only one
Under the sun!

BALLAD.

THERE on the sea sand
Of the salt lagoon
My true love passed me by
Under the moon.

She passed me by so close
I could have touched her hand,
I could have called her name,
There on the sea sand.

Sky blue her robe;
It brushed my cloak of gray.
We said not a word,
With all the words to say.

There we passed groping
Where the water nears.
Her eyes were blind with judgment,
And mine with tears.

There on the sea sand
Of the salt lagoon
My true love passed me by
Under the moon.

TO A STARFISH.

WHY thou art here with "simple ignorance"
We might have mused upon in other days,—
If out of heaven to resounding ways
Thou fleddest what the wrath of gods might chance,
If deeply jewelled in five-pointed dance
Outstayed sea-crowning of Calypso's praise,
Or lost when Pleiads swam the ocean maze.
Yet thanks to science' infinite romance
We know exactly now why thou art here;
The oyster-bed preceding, like a bow
Thou comest curved and ready, even so,
With belly turned to suck the oysters near,
Which great and small the varied reasons are
Why thou art here, ethereal little star!

CHANGING RUNNERS.

TRAILING along the wet sea sand
And through the valley it is borne,
And in the woods the burning brand
Seems now advancing, now withdrawn
As the swift, flagging feet come on
To one that waits half up the height
With muscles tightening; the light
Dips as it passes from hand to hand,
And over the mountain the torch is gone!

FREE-THINKERS.

We shake the night with onset, the gale is in our faces.
On through night, through the night we ride.
Earth cries out from hid and omened places,
Secrets waken in cave, moraine and tide.
On through night, through the night we ride.

Back-blown flare of windy torch-light traces
For Columbus the isles that he descried.
Men of honor, leave the land's embraces,
Gold and fountain leave for those who died!
On through night, through the night we ride.

Down earth's end unfathomable spaces
Wait. Experience, cowering, turns to hide.
Hell yawns under the forward-beating paces,
Crystal spheres* are shattered far and wide.
On through night, through the night we ride.

Rest we ask not, nor the good earth's graces,
Earth whom we to thousand suns allied.
Goal we know not. Deepest night encases
Heaven the road, and hell the road denied.
On through night, through the night we ride.

*That is, the Ptolemaic theory of the spheres.

ABELARD.

WITHOUT,—dull sky and howling sea,
And the head of St. Gildas' savage abbey,
Wrapped in thought as man can be,
Pacing his cloister absently;
Within,—the mutinous gray monks, met
Where no taper ever raised
The blackness of the oubliette,
Whisper, raging and amazed,
How the lethal dish, though set
For Abelard, had missed its way.
They could only watch and pray.
He might yet be graveward sent
With poison in the Sacrament.
And Abelard, the golden tongue
Of student Paris and Corbeil,
Guide of the insurgent young,
By Soissons Synod forced to lay
His book on fire, for that they
Smelt Sabellian heresy,—
Abelard, who ever taught
The fierce integrity of thought,
Walks his cloister musingly.
But he does not think on these,
Nor on peerless Héloïse
Single-souled enough to win
Triumph at love's wakeful throne.
Halfway love made his love sin.
Piety he madly cast
Over the exhausted past,
A cloak like parchment dry and thin.
He is true to thought alone.
So he paces, challenging the dead.
Augustine spake sooth? But St. Paul said
Quite the opposite; if Gregory
Wrote by inspiration, then Jerome
Wrote by something else; they disagree.
Athanasius here and Isidore
There—a contradiction—*Sic et Non.*

Heeding not love's scourge and doom's
Behind, while cloudily before
Excommunication looms,
He walks his cloister musingly.

THE UNDETERRED.

Child:

I ride to meet the globèd moon tonight
A charger, swimming, through a snow-white rack,
The amber ring and spiritual blue.

Sister:

Beautiful child, the fairy steeds run wide
Upon their pasturage of broom, to seek
Immeasurable pools that rise and fall.

Child:

I ride to meet the orange moon tonight
A stallion, wingèd as I dare not tell.
I think his mane streams like an angry sun.

Sister:

Beloved of music, Pegasus flies free
And proud, with heroes; far from our dim earth
His hoofs are on the oriental hills.

Child:

And now the wind is carrying more high
My thistledown-light words so chill and high.
I ride tonight the pale horse they call Death.

THE ANTIQUE NECKLACE.

THE snake I clasp round my throat was chosen
 By one I love who had first loved me,
The golden snake, with his red eyes frozen
As gems upcast by a sanguine sea,
The golden snake, with his magic olden
 As Thebes may be.

For him full many a slave was stranger
To sun and life in the far-hewn mine,
And he has looked like a living danger
On warlike Pharaohs laid in line.
I tremble, knowing his scales resemble
 The dead spears' shine.

At night, when all of the world reposes,
I dream the darkness begins to gleam,
And smoothly strangling, the reptile closes
About my throat in a gliding stream
That brightens fast as the necklace tightens,
 Within my dream.

VENICE.

THE dews of a glittering midnight have lain on my hair,
 And the courts gape wide from their moony mirrors cold
While I hold my breath for an echo upon the stair,
Awaiting the clangèd armour, the ring and the gold,
Awaiting the preluding of an ancient air.
Will they tell as they long ago told me that yet I am fair?
For I dreamed in a slanderous dream of the woes of the old,
And the dews of a glittering midnight have lain on my hair.

VAGABOND.

A WILD rose, closed from night and rain,
I kissed as I came over the plain.
May she sleep and dream again
How one who'll roam
Till the clouds come home
Kissed her, laughing, in the rain.

APRIL AFTERNOON.

THE wingèd leaves are too transparent bright
For shadow on the ground. The sun pours through
Swamp maple's ghostly grayness to delight
Of the moist earth, where hushed anemones
And wakeful starflowers hoard their early dew,
And woolly ferns uncurl at roots of trees.
A brook finds out its journey cold and new
Through leaf mould and deep mossy crevices.

NATURE SPEAKS.

I CALL in wind and heavenly flame
And in the sea
For girls that never come again to me.
All my children in the spring
Have another wakening
Save these, that never come again to me.
These, that full of wildest glee
Swayed in the tree-tops, ran against the blast,
These that not ever time nor fear could tame
Love tamed at last.

THE NORTH WIND.

I HEAR the north wind plunging to a goal
That he knows not,—
The formless one, the nameless one, the unforgot,
Beyond the arctic or antarctic pole.
I hear him howling anger up the night
Because a windowpane arrests his flight
With form, and, manifest, the journey breaks.
A stream, a cliff, a branchy wood he makes,
Clanging his wings in anger at the sight,
Detained from warfare with the infinite;
In anger and in terror from the spot
Flies to the formless one, flies to the nameless one, the unforgot,
Lessening along the night
To what is not.

ADVICE.

HOLD thy life a wingèd seed
Blowing o'er the good earth's mead.
Toss it an thou list, nor rue it.
Wilt thou not? Then time will do it.

Hold thy name a cockle boat
That the seaward rivers float.
Let the river waves leap through it.
Wilt thou not? Then time will do it.

Hold thy love but as a light
Flying through a windy night.
Let the sporting winds pursue it.
Wilt thou not? Then time will do it.

THE EAGLE'S FLIGHT.

WINGS go through the night, outspeeding earth toward dawn.
After many hours the night is moved to speak:
"What are you, solitary eagle?"
"The thought of man."
"Eagle, your wings are blackened with old flame."
"From the temples of Hathor at Denderah I beheld Eltanin rise."
"Where in illimitable space might be your eyrie?"
"The eyrie is illimitable space."

ALI TO AZRAEL.

Out of the Wilderness.

Angel that ever leanest at the portal
Above the shell where lustral water lies
Deeper than depth of the reflected eyes
That are not mortal,

I front my death. The liberating hour
Is come. I sought and never found reply,—
In tortured consciousness and baffled power
Forgotten, die.

A stranger that has offered to thy heaven
Spare vintaging of earth grown wise too late,
A watcher of the planets that are seven
Turns to thy gate.

I strove with beasts, expatriate and lonely.
My fault was great, and great mine agony.
I never called light darkness. For this only
Pray unto thee.

At length, before untried abysms cover
Insentience, reconciling clod with clod,
An instant come to me as to thy lover,
Angel of God!

LITANY OF THE COMFORTABLE.

Remembering Thy sacrificial throne,
We chosen guardians of revelation
Establish on the earth the Word's foundation
On men that groan.

We praise and magnify Thee, that of seed
Thy martyrs planted who in anguish died
We are the fruit indeed,
Consummate, justified.

Against inquiry and ardour's heat
Thy mercy we entreat;

From consequence untoward and perilous
Deliver us;

From rod and tribulation for Thy sake
Deliver us;

From slander, ruin and from social break
Deliver us;

From too-exceeding love and penitence;
From unproductive forms of violence
Deliver us;

From needless pain and execrated sorrow;
From the fool's paradise, unplanned tomorrow;
From hunger fell, with its fell partner thirst;
From leprous blight of poverty accursed;
From exile, revolution and the rest
That Thou hast blest,
Deliver us;

And at the last, we pray Thee, of Thy grace
From sudden death
Deliver us;
Lest it be truly as the prophet saith,
That in unsheltered space
We look upon Thy face.

CONCERNING MARTYRDOM.

ONE man views uncreated light;
The crowd descends to raging night.
One man forgives; the multitude
Reeks of hate and fear and blood.
Can a man be free indeed
When his brothers are not freed,
Or the Kingdom be possessed
When the mob at madness' heat
Changes to a preying beast?
Martyrdom is incomplete.
It is but the link between
What shall be and what has been.
Men saw justice rude begun
When evil was for evil done;
Then the martyr's sacrifice
With good for evil made them wise,
Being but the stepping-stone
To the greater justice shown
Of good exchanged for good alone.
When the multitude become
Nobly wise and calmly free
There will be no martyrdom,
Only reciprocity
Of good interchanged for good
And difference largely understood.
Sacrifice leads into this,
New law with ancient law to blend,
And eternal justice is
The beginning and the end.

ELAN VITAL.

SOME days I tend with careful sun and showers,
But hungry time demands their fruit of me,
And I alone possess my wasted hours,
Which are the children of infinity.
I dare rejoice that I have offered gifts
To many a deity of wood and clay,
And many a house have built where sea sand drifts,
And many a ship lost on the ocean-way.
I dare rejoice at trespassing and tears
And at the doomed Niagaras of the soul
That, flowing faster as the chasm nears,
Go down in thunder, knowing not their goal;
For by their depth of wastage I can tell
How deep the source, how inexhaustible.